# Stone Soup

Written by
Cath Jones

Illustrated by
Finn Dean

A traveller came marching down a track. The sun was setting and there was snow on the ground.

She spied a line of huts with flickering lights in the windows.

She tapped on the window of the first hut and a man stuck out his head.

"It's cold and I have travelled a long way. Could you let me have a bit of food for my supper?" she asked.

The man had lots of food, but he said, "We had a bad harvest this year. We don't have any food at all."

The traveller tapped at each hut in turn. She felt the eyes of people looking out at her.

But each time the reply was the same. "We have no food."

I will play a little trick on the people in the huts, she thought.

"I am sad that you too have no food," the traveller told them. "I will make stone soup for all of us to eat."

"What is stone soup?" the people asked.

"It's not anything mystical," said the traveller. "Lend me a big soup pot. All I need to make stone soup is water and my stone."

She took a stone from her pocket and popped it into the pot of water.

Plop!

Soon, the water in the soup pot was hot. The traveller took a spoon and sipped some of her stone soup.

"Well?" the people asked.

The traveller shrugged her shoulders. "Yum," she said, "but it would be better with a carrot in it."

"I have carrots in my hut!" a man said. He ran to his hut and chopped the carrots. Then he popped them into the soup pot.

"Much better!" the traveller said. "But if I could add a potato, it would be better still."

And so it went on.

Each time the traveller sipped the soup, she asked for a different food.

Did they have any turnips, or any potatoes, or any tomatoes?

Each time, someone would run and get the food and pop it into the pot.

Soon, mouth-watering smells drifted up into the sky.

The people licked their lips.

"That stone soup smells good!" they said. "When can we try it?"

"Bring benches and blankets," the traveller said. "Then we can all eat."

The traveller and the people ate all the soup.

"Yum," said all the people. "Stone soup is fantastic!"

The next day, the traveller left at sunrise. She left behind a little gift for the people.

It was a stone, for them to make their own stone soup.